The President's Framework for Business Tax Reform

Contents

I0428620

Introduction 1

I. Cut Loopholes and Subsidies, Broaden the Base, and Cut the Corporate Tax Rate 2

II. Strengthen American Manufacturing and Innovation 11

III. Strengthen the International Tax System to Encourage Domestic Investment........ 13

IV. Simplify and Cut Taxes for America's Small Businesses.. 16

V. Restore Fiscal Responsibility 18

APPENDIX I: Statutory Tax Rate Versus Effective Tax Rate in the United States........... 19

APPENDIX II: Effective Marginal Tax Rates Including Individual Income Taxes 22

Introduction

America's system of business taxation is in need of reform. The United States has a relatively narrow corporate tax base compared to other countries—a tax base reduced by loopholes, tax expenditures, and tax planning. This is combined with a statutory corporate tax rate that will soon be the highest among advanced countries. As a result of this combination of a relatively narrow tax base and a high statutory tax rate, the U.S. tax system is uncompetitive and inefficient. The system distorts choices such as where to produce, what to invest in, how to finance a business, and what business form to use. And it does too little to encourage job creation and investment in the United States while allowing firms to benefit from incentives to locate production and shift profits overseas. The system is also too complicated—especially for America's small businesses.

For these reasons, the President is committed to reform that will support the competitiveness of American businesses—large and small—and increase incentives to invest and hire in the United States by lowering rates, cutting tax expenditures, and reducing complexity, while being fiscally responsible.

This report presents the President's Framework for business tax reform. In laying out this Framework, the President recognizes that tax reform will take time, require work on a bipartisan basis, and benefit from additional feedback from stakeholders and experts. To start that process, this report outlines what the President believes should be five key elements of business tax reform.

PRESIDENT OBAMA'S FIVE ELEMENTS OF BUSINESS TAX REFORM

I. **Eliminate dozens of tax loopholes and subsidies, broaden the base and cut the corporate tax rate to spur growth in America:** The Framework would eliminate dozens of different tax expenditures and fundamentally reform the business tax base to reduce distortions that hurt productivity and growth. It would reinvest these savings to lower the corporate tax rate to 28 percent, putting the United States in line with major competitor countries and encouraging greater investment in America.

II. **Strengthen American manufacturing and innovation:** The Framework would refocus the manufacturing deduction and use the savings to reduce the effective rate on manufacturing to no more than 25 percent, while encouraging greater research and development and the production of clean energy.

III. **Strengthen the international tax system, including establishing a new minimum tax on foreign earnings, to encourage domestic investment:** Our tax system should not give companies an incentive to locate production overseas or engage in accounting games to shift profits abroad, eroding the U.S. tax base. Introducing a minimum tax on foreign earnings would help address these problems and discourage a global race to the bottom in tax rates.

IV. **Simplify and cut taxes for America's small businesses:** Tax reform should make tax filing simpler for small businesses and entrepreneurs so that they can focus on growing their businesses rather than filling out tax returns.

V. **Restore fiscal responsibility and not add a dime to the deficit:** Business tax reform should be fully paid for and lead to greater fiscal responsibility than our current business tax system by either eliminating or making permanent and fully paying for temporary tax provisions now in the tax code.

I. Cut Loopholes and Subsidies, Broaden the Base, and Cut the Corporate Tax Rate

The United States now essentially trades off greater tax expenditures, loopholes, and tax planning for a higher statutory corporate tax rate relative to other countries. This is a poor trade that produces a tax system that is uncompetitive relative to other countries, distorts business decision making, and slows economic growth.

In recent years, our major trading partners have overhauled their tax codes, lowered their statutory corporate tax rates, and in some cases broadened their tax bases. The United States has not enacted similar reforms, leaving the United States with the second highest statutory tax rate among advanced countries. In April 2012, after the scheduled reductions in Japanese tax rates go into effect, the United States will have the highest statutory corporate income tax rate in the Organization for Economic Cooperation and Development (OECD).

Figure 1 compares the statutory corporate tax rate in the United States to the GDP-weighted average rate in other OECD countries, including sub-national (such as state and local) corporate taxes where relevant. In 1986, the United States lowered its statutory tax rate to well below the average for other OECD countries. Since the late 1980s, however, many OECD countries have reduced statutory corporate tax rates so that the U.S. rate now exceeds the OECD average. In 2011, the U.S. statutory corporate income tax rate was 39.2 percent (including an average effective state and local combined rate of 4.2 percent in addition to the federal rate of 35 percent). That is over 11 percentage points higher than the weighted average statutory rate in other OECD countries (27.8 percent), almost 7 percentage points higher than the weighted average statutory rate in other G-7 countries (32.3 percent), and second only to Japan which is scheduled to lower its rate below the U.S. rate in April 2012 (see Table 1).[1]

The difference in statutory corporate tax rates between the United States and other advanced countries will further widen this year. For example, this year, the federal corporate income tax rate in Canada has decreased by 1.5 percentage points. In April, the United Kingdom is scheduled reduce its corporate tax rate by 1 percentage point, and, that same month, Japan will reduce its national corporate tax rate by 1.5 percentage points.

However, even as the United States has among the highest statutory corporate tax rates, the effective marginal tax rate on corporate investment in the United States is similar to that in other competitor countries (see Table 1). The effective marginal rate represents what businesses would actually expect to pay on a marginal investment. The discrepancy between where the United States ranks in terms of the statutory rate and in terms of the effective marginal rate comes about for a number of reasons. These include the United States having a narrower tax base—reduced by tax expenditures, loopholes, and tax planning—and the presence of other, higher taxes (such as property taxes) imposed on corporations in competitor countries. (For a full discussion comparing the U.S. statutory tax rate and average effective tax rate to those in other countries, see Appendix I.)

---

[1] The U.S. statutory corporate tax rate does not reflect the domestic production activities deduction, which effectively provides a lower rate for corporations with qualifying activities. This deduction is discussed in more detail below.

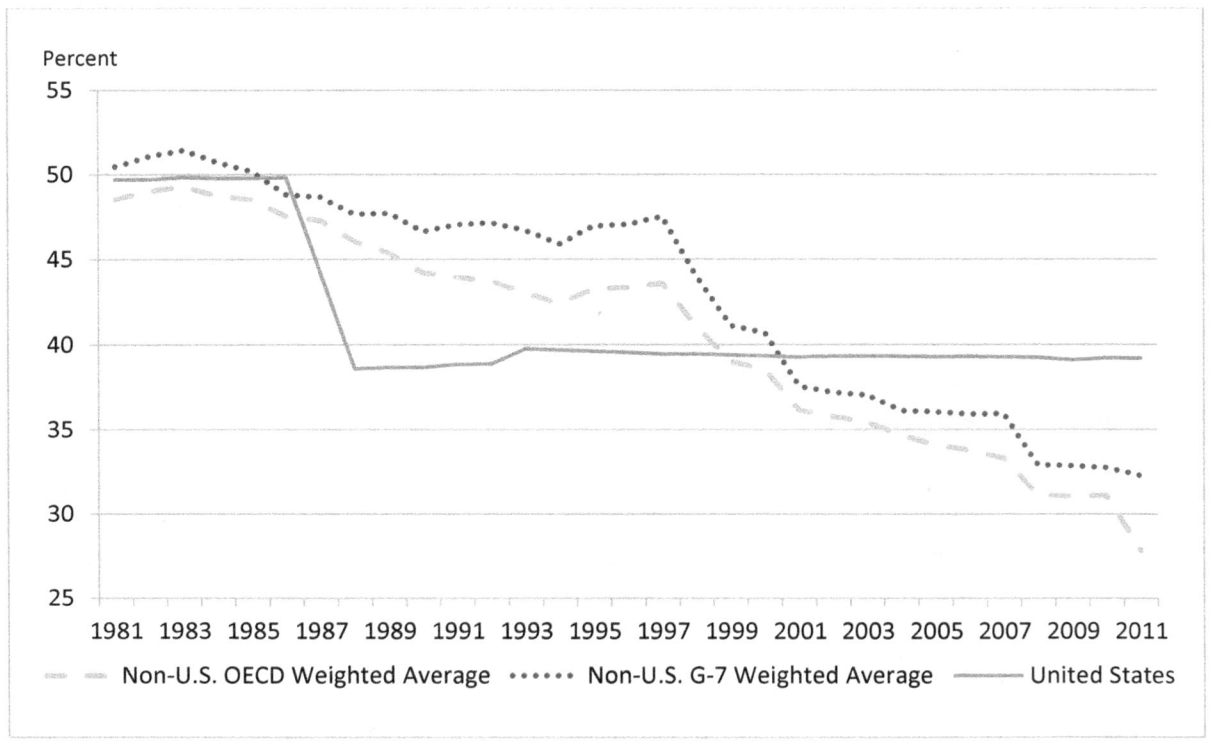

TABLE 1: 2011 G-7 STATUTORY CORPORATE TAX RATES (IN PERCENT)

Country	Statutory Corporate Tax Rate (including subnational taxes)	Effective Marginal Tax Rate (including subnational taxes)[b]
Canada	27.6	33.0
France	34.4	28.3
Germany	30.2	23.3
Italy	31.3	24.0
Japan	39.5	42.9
United Kingdom	26.0	32.3
United States	39.2	29.2
G-7 average excluding the U.S.[a]	**32.3**	**31.9**

[a.] *The G-7 Average is calculated using 2010 gross domestic product (in current US dollars) as weights. Source: OECD.*

[b.] *See Table A1 in Appendix I for an explanation of the methodology for calculating the effective marginal tax rate.*

While the United States is generally in line with competitor countries when it comes to the overall average level of taxes paid on corporate investments, this is not an argument against reform; in fact, it is an argument and motivation for reform. The trade-off of a higher statutory tax rate in exchange for a narrower tax base with numerous loopholes and subsidies is a poor one.

The tax preferences created by tax expenditures and loopholes add complexity to the tax system and contribute to a substantial business tax compliance burden. Additional rules and regulations are needed to limit incentives to their intended beneficiaries. Taxpayers have to spend time and money learning about tax incentives and often rely on third parties to help them navigate the thicket of complex tax rules. The Internal Revenue Service (IRS) has to spend resources monitoring and enforcing the rules. Disputes invariably arise between the IRS and taxpayers, and society expends resources adjudicating these disputes. In fact, it is estimated that the administrative and compliance costs in the corporate income tax system now exceed $40 billion per year, or more than 12 percent of revenue collected.[2]

Moreover, the tax expenditures and loopholes in the U.S. tax system, together with the structure of the corporate tax system, produce significant distortions that can result in a less efficient allocation of capital, reducing the productive capacity of the economy and U.S. living standards. The distortions created by the tax system are explored further below.

(i)   Distorting the form of investment by industry and asset type.

Currently, tax expenditures in the tax code vary dramatically by industry. These differences manifest themselves in disparate average tax rates across industries. Table 2 shows effective actual federal corporate tax rates by industry in 2007-2008. The overall average federal tax rate for U.S. corporations was 26 percent—well below the federal statutory rate of 35 percent. Within that average, there was considerable variation by industry—from a low of a 14 percent average tax rate for utilities to a 31 percent average tax rate for construction.[3]

Tax preferences also lead to very different effective marginal tax rates across assets. For example, because of accelerated depreciation and other features of the tax code, in 2005 income from a typical investment in structures for oil and gas faced an effective total marginal tax rate (including corporate and investor level taxes) of about 9 percent as compared to a 32 percent rate for manufacturing buildings.[4]

The result is a tax system that distorts investment decisions. By allocating capital inefficiently, this system lowers living standards now[5] and could also impede technological innovation. The pace of innovation is a key determinant of economic growth, and innovation tends to be directly related to those areas in which we make capital investments. Firms do not reap the benefits of technological advances until new capital is brought into production. Given this interplay between innovation and capital accumulation, the distortions created by the current corporate income tax may slow economic growth over the long term.

---

[2] PRESIDENT'S ECONOMIC RECOVERY ADVISORY BOARD, REPORT ON TAX REFORM OPTIONS: SIMPLIFICATION, COMPLIANCE, AND CORPORATE TAXATION 65 (2010). In a review of the literature, the Government Accountability Office makes a similar finding. GAO describes two studies that find that the cost of compliance for all businesses (corporations and partnerships) was $40 billion to $80 billion per year as of the early 2000s. GOV'T ACCOUNTABILITY OFFICE, GAO-05-878, SUMMARY OF ESTIMATES OF THE COSTS OF THE FEDERAL TAX SYSTEM 14 tbl.3 (2005).

[3] Calculations of the Treasury Office of Tax Analysis.

[4] CONG. BUDGET OFFICE, TAXING CAPITAL INCOME: EFFECTIVE RATES AND APPROACHES TO REFORM 10-11 tbl.2 (2005).

[5] See, e.g., Alan J. Auerbach and Kevin Hassett, *Tax Policy and Business Fixed Investment in the United States*, 47 J. Pub. Econ. 141 (1992); Dale W. Jorgenson and Kun-Young Yun, *Tax Policy and Capital Allocation*, 88 SCANDINAVIAN J. ECON. 355 (1986).

TABLE 2: EFFECTIVE ACTUAL FEDERAL CORPORATE TAX RATES BY INDUSTRY FOR 2007 – 2008

Industry	Effective Actual Corporate Tax Rate
Agriculture, Forestry, Fishing and Hunting	22%
Mining	18%
Utilities	14%
Construction	31%
Manufacturing	26%
Wholesale and Retail Trade	31%
Transportation and Warehousing	19%
Information	25%
Insurance	25%
Finance and Holding Companies	28%
Real Estate	23%
Leasing	18%
All Services	29%
Average Effective Actual Tax Rate	**26%**

Source: U.S. Department of the Treasury, Office of Tax Analysis

(ii)   Distorting the financing of investment.

The current corporate tax code encourages corporations to finance themselves with debt rather than with equity. Specifically, under the current tax code, corporate dividends are not deductible from corporate taxable income, but interest payments are. This disparity creates a sizable wedge in the effective tax rates applied to returns from investments financed with equity versus debt. Profits generated by an equity-financed investment will be taxed at the 35 percent corporate rate, leaving 65 percent of the profits for dividend payments to shareholders. In contrast, profits from the same investment funded by debt will only be taxed to the extent they exceed the associated interest payments. Once the deductibility of interest is combined with accelerated depreciation, the cost of debt capital declines even further. In fact, on average, debt-financed investments are subsidized (i.e., their effective marginal tax rate is negative), as income generated by such investments is more than offset by deductions for interest and accelerated depreciation.

For example, the effective corporate marginal tax rate on new equity-financed investment in equipment is 37 percent in the United States. At the same time, the effective marginal tax rate on the same investment made with debt financing is *minus* 60 percent—a gap of 97 percentage points. This compares to an average difference of about 51 percentage points for other G-7 countries (see Table 3).[6]

This tax preference for debt financing has important macroeconomic consequences. First and foremost, outsized reliance on debt financing can increase the risk of financial distress and thus raise the likelihood of bankruptcy. Unlike equity financing, which can flexibly absorb corporate losses, debt and the associated contractual covenants require ongoing payments of interest and principal and allow creditors to force a firm into bankruptcy. A solvent firm with limited liquidity that is struggling to make its debt payments may experience losses of customers, suppliers, and employees. It may engage in

---

[6] Calculations of the Treasury Office of Tax Analysis.

destructive asset "fire sales" and forgo economically profitable investments. And, in an attempt to avoid bankruptcy, levered firms faced with financial distress may resort to high-risk negative economic value investments. In the broader context, a large bias towards debt financing in the corporate tax code may lead to greater aggregate leverage and the associated firm-level and macroeconomic costs of debt financing.[7]

TABLE 3: EFFECTIVE MARGINAL TAX RATES FOR DEBT AND EQUITY FINANCED CORPORATE INVESTMENTS: SELECTED OECD COUNTRIES

Country	Effective Marginal Tax Rate Equipment (Equity)	Effective Marginal Tax Rate Equipment (Debt)	Difference
Australia	31	-23	-54
Austria	27	-14	-41
Belgium	5	-50	-55
Canada	28	-21	-49
Finland	27	-18	-45
France	29	-59	-88
Germany	32	-10	-42
Greece	14	-26	-40
Ireland	15	-4	-19
Italy	38	1	-37
Japan	49	-4	-53
Netherlands	27	-14	-41
Norway	33	-11	-43
Portugal	22	-34	-56
Spain	36	-22	-58
Sweden	24	-24	-48
Switzerland	22	-18	-40
UK	30	-9	-40
United States	37	-60	-97
Average, Excluding U.S. (unweighted)	34	-17	-51
G-7 Average, Excluding U.S. (unweighted)	37	-15	-51

Source: U.S. Department of Treasury, Office of Tax Analysis.

See notes to Table 1: G-7 Statutory and Effective Corporate Tax Rates (in Percent): 2011. Averages are calculated using 2010 gross domestic product (in current U.S. dollars) as weights

---

[7] See, e.g., RUUD A. DE MOOJ, INT'L MONETARY FUND, TAX BIASES TO DEBT FINANCE: ASSESSING THE PROBLEM, FINDING SOLUTIONS (2011); Joel Slemrod, *Lessons for Tax Policy in the Great Recession*, 62 NAT'L TAX J. 387 (2009).

(iii) Distorting the form of businesses.

Business may be organized under a variety of different forms, including C-corporations, S-corporations, partnerships, and sole-proprietorships. These organizational forms offer varying legal, regulatory, and tax treatments. The primary difference in tax treatment between C-corporations, on the one hand, and S-corporations, partnerships, and sole-proprietorships, on the other, is applicability of the corporate income tax. C-corporations are subject to the corporate tax, while pass-through entities are not. (These other entities are known as "pass through" because profits pass through to the individual without being taxed at the entity level.)

The combined effect of this varying tax treatment has contributed to a lower effective tax rate for pass-through entities relative to C-corporations. The effective marginal tax rate on new investment by C-corporations is now 32.3 percent, while the effective marginal tax rate on new investment by pass-through businesses 26.4 percent.[8]

As a result, large companies are increasingly avoiding corporate tax liability by organizing themselves as pass-through businesses. Pass-through businesses represented less than one quarter of net business income in 1980, but more than 70 percent of net business income in 2008—the most recent year for which data are available (see Table 4).[9] While the pattern from year-to-year can be volatile, the overall trend is clear.

The ability of large pass-through entities to take advantage of preferential tax treatment has placed businesses organizing as C-corporations at a disadvantage. By allowing large pass-through entities preferential treatment, the tax code distorts choices of organizational form, which can lead to losses in economic efficiency; business managers should make choices about organizational form based on criteria other than tax treatment.[10]

(iv) Distortions in favor of shifting production and profits overseas.

A higher statutory rate can encourage corporations to shift income and production out of the United States to a lower tax jurisdiction, especially in today's global marketplace. The gain from shifting a dollar of income from one jurisdiction to another equals the difference in statutory tax rates between the two locations. The statutory rate may also affect the decision to invest in one country rather than another, especially where the investments are independent and highly profitable. This is particularly true for earnings and production that cannot benefit from special deductions and tax credits.

The empirical evidence suggests that income-shifting behavior by multinational corporations is a significant concern that should be addressed through tax reform.[11] The pre-tax profitability of controlled foreign corporations is negatively correlated with local country statutory tax rates, taking into account real economic factors such as financial structure, capital employed, and other non-

---

[8] Calculations of the Treasury Office of Tax Analysis.

[9] Internal Revenue Service, Statistics of Income, *available at* www.irs.gov/taxstats.

[10] *See, e.g.*, Austan Goolsbee, *The Impact Of The Corporate Income Tax: Evidence From State Organizational Form Data*, 88 J. Pub. Econ. 2283 (2004); Jeffrey K. Mackie-Mason and Roger H. Gordon, *How Much Do Taxes Discourage Incorporation?* 52 J. Fin. 477 (1997); Roger H. Gordon, and Jeffrey Mackie-Mason, *Tax Distortions to the Choice of Organizational Form*, 55 J. Pub. Econ. 279 (1994).

[11] *See, e.g.*, Eric J. Bartelsmana and Roel M.W.J. Beetsma, Why Pay More? Corporate Tax Avoidance Through Transfer Pricing in OECD Countries, 87 J. PUB. ECON 2225 (2003); Edward D. Kleinbard, *Stateless Income*, 11 FLA. TAX REV. 699 (2011).

transfer pricing operational aspects of multinational groups.[12] In addition to the evidence that companies generally shift income from high-tax foreign countries to low-tax foreign countries, there is also evidence of income shifting specifically from the United States to other countries.[13] Income shifting from the United States to other countries significantly erodes the U.S. tax base and leads to lower corporate tax receipts. Evidence suggests that high statutory tax rates may also affect a company's willingness to locate in the United States following mergers and acquisitions.[14]

TABLE 4: SHARES OF TOTAL BUSINESS RETURNS, RECEIPTS, AND NET INCOME – 1980 TO 2008

	1980	1990	2000	2008
S Corporations				
Returns	4%	8%	11%	13%
Total Receipts	3%	13%	15%	18%
Net Income (less deficit)	1%	10%	17%	22%
Partnerships [a]				
Returns	11%	8%	8%	10%
Total Receipts	4%	4%	10%	14%
Net Income (less deficit)	3%	4%	22%	32%
Sole Proprietorships				
Returns	69%	74%	72%	72%
Total Receipts	6%	6%	4%	4%
Net Income (less deficit)	18%	30%	18%	19%
C Corporations [b]				
Returns	17%	11%	9%	6%
Total Receipts	87%	77%	71%	64%
Net Income (less deficit)	78%	57%	43%	27%

a Includes LLC & LLPs
b Excludes 1120-RIC and 1120 REIT
Source: Internal Revenue Service, Statistics of Income, www.irs.gov/taxstats

---

[12] See, for example, the review of the literature in DEPT. OF THE TREAS., REPORT TO THE CONGRESS ON EARNINGS STRIPPING, TRANSFER PRICING AND U.S. INCOME TAX TREATIES ch.3 (2007) and Jane Gravelle, *Tax Havens: International Tax Avoidance and Evasion*, 62 NATIONAL TAX JOURNAL 727 (2009).

[13] Harry Grubert, *Foreign Taxes and the Growing Share of Multinational Company Income Abroad: Profits, Not Sales, Are Being Globalized*, NAT'L TAX J. (forthcoming 2012).

[14] Harry Huizinga and Johannes Voget, *International Taxation and the Direction and Volume of Cross Border M&A*, 64 J. FIN. 1217 (2009).

The President's Framework would eliminate dozens of different tax expenditures and fundamentally reform the business tax base to reduce distortions that hurt productivity and growth. It would reinvest the savings in reducing the rate from 35 percent to 28 percent. This combination of a broader base and a lower rate would alleviate a number of the significant economic distortions identified above that cause businesses to base investment decisions on tax rules rather than economic returns. Furthermore, this would encourage greater investment here at home and reduce incentives for U.S. companies to move their operations abroad or to shift profits to lower-tax jurisdictions. Where appropriate, the changes would allow adequate transition periods to permit affected parties to adjust to the new permanent tax rules. Finally, this reform would bring certainty to a business tax code that annually features the expiration of dozens of business tax incentives. Many of these temporary provisions would be eliminated and those that remain would be made permanent—helping to improve incentives to allocate capital efficiently and to simplify the tax code.

Specifically, the President's Framework would:

- **Reduce the corporate tax rate from 35 percent to 28 percent**. This reduction in the rate would put the United States in line with other advanced countries, help encourage greater investment in the United States, and reduce the tax-related economic distortions discussed above.

- **Eliminate dozens of business tax loopholes and tax expenditures.** The President's plan would start from a presumption that we should eliminate all tax expenditures for specific industries, with the few exceptions that are critical to broader growth or fairness. The following are a few examples of specific reductions in tax expenditures and loophole closers that should be part of any reform:

  - *Eliminate "last in first out" accounting.* Under the "last-in, first-out" (LIFO) method of accounting for inventories, it is assumed that the cost of the items of inventory that are sold is equal to the cost of the items of inventory that were most recently purchased or produced. This allows some businesses to artificially lower their tax liability. The Framework would end LIFO, bringing us in line with international standards and simplifying the tax system.

  - *Eliminate oil and gas tax preferences.* The tax code currently subsidizes oil and gas production through tax expenditures that provide preferences for these industries over others. The Framework would repeal tax preferences available for fossil fuels. This includes, for instance, repealing the expensing of intangible drilling costs, a provision that allows oil companies to immediately write-off these costs rather than recovering the cost over time as for most capital investments in other industries. This also includes repealing percentage depletion for oil and natural gas wells, which allows certain oil producers and royalty owners to recover the cost of oil and gas wells based on a percentage of the income they earn from selling oil and gas from the property rather than on the exhaustion of the property. Percentage depletion allows deductions that can exceed the cost of the property.

  - *Reform treatment of insurance industry and products.* The tax code currently allows insurance to be used as a form of tax shelter for major corporations. In particular, corporations can invest in life insurance for their officers, directors, or employees, benefit from "inside build up" (gains on that investment) that are tax-deferred or never taxed, and finance that investment through debt that allows the corporation to take interest deductions earlier than any gain realized on the life insurance. The Framework would close this loophole and not allow interest deductions allocable to life insurance policies unless the contract is on an officer, director, or employee who is at least a 20 percent owner of the business. The Framework would also make a number of other reforms to the treatment of insurance companies and products to improve information reporting, simplify tax treatment, and close loopholes.

- *Taxing carried (profits) interests as ordinary income.* Currently, many hedge fund managers, private equity partners, and other managers in partnerships are able to pay a 15 percent capital gains rate on their labor income (on income that is known as "carried interest"). This tax loophole is inappropriate and allows these financial managers to pay a lower tax rate on their income than other workers. The Framework would eliminate the loophole for managers in investment services partnerships and tax carried interest at ordinary income rates.

- *Eliminate special depreciation rules for corporate purchases of aircraft.* This would eliminate the special depreciation rules that allow owners of non-commercial aircraft to depreciate their aircraft more quickly (over five years) than commercial aircraft (seven years).

- **Reform the corporate tax base to invest savings in cutting the tax rate and reducing harmful distortions.** This Framework lays out a menu of options that should be under consideration in reform. At least several of these would be necessary to get the rate down to 28 percent:

  - *Addressing depreciation schedules.* Current depreciation schedules generally overstate the true economic depreciation of assets. Although this provides an incentive to invest, it comes at the cost of higher tax rates for a given amount of revenue. In an increasingly global economy, accelerated depreciation may be a less effective way to increase investment and job creation than reinvesting the savings from moving towards economic depreciation into reducing tax rates.

  - *Reducing the bias toward debt financing.* A lower corporate tax rate by itself would automatically reduce but not eliminate the bias toward debt financing. Additional steps like reducing the deductibility of interest for corporations should be considered as part of a reform plan. This is because a tax system that is more neutral towards debt and equity will reduce incentives to overleverage and produce more stable business finances, especially in times of economic stress. In addition, reducing the deductibility of interest for corporations could finance lower tax rates and do more to encourage investment in the United States than keeping rates higher or paying for the rate reductions in other ways.

  - *Establishing greater parity between large corporations and large non-corporate counterparts.* Establishing greater parity between large corporations and their large non-corporate counterparts should be considered as a way to help improve equity, reduce distortions in how businesses organize themselves, and finance lower tax rates. A variety of ways to do this have been proposed, including ones discussed in the 2005 report of President Bush's Advisory Panel on Tax Reform,[15] and in reform options developed by President Obama's Economic Recovery Advisory Board in 2010.[16] It is essential that any changes in this area should not affect small businesses.

- **Improve transparency and reduce accounting gimmicks.** Corporate tax reform should increase transparency and reduce the gap between book income, reported to shareholders, and taxable income, reported to the IRS. These reforms could include greater disclosure of annual corporate income tax payments.

---

[15] President's Advisory Panel on Tax Reform, Simple, Fair, and Pro-Growth: Proposals to Fix America's Tax System 129 (2005).

[16] President's Economic Recovery Advisory Board, *supra* note 2, at 74-77.

II. Strengthen American Manufacturing and Innovation

The manufacturing sector plays an outsized role in the U.S. economy with significant spillovers to other sectors that make it particularly important to future job creation, innovation, and economic growth. Furthermore, the United States is in a global competition for manufacturing investment, and both existing and emerging manufacturing industries are subject to more intense international competition than other sectors.

Encouraging manufacturing investment and production supports higher wage jobs.[17] Manufacturing contributes disproportionately to U.S. innovation; manufacturing firms conduct more than two-thirds of the private sector research and development (R&D) in the United States and employ the majority of scientists and engineers in the private sector.[18] Investment in new production capacity and proximity to the manufacturing process create spillovers across firms and industries, leading to the ideas, capabilities, and technologies that enable innovation. In this way, investments in manufacturing increase innovation and economy-wide productivity growth.[19] In addition, manufacturing accounts for nearly 60 percent of total exports[20] and can help address our current account deficit.

R&D is especially important for manufacturing, which is a technology-intensive sector. In the 1980s, the United States was the leader in providing tax incentives for R&D through the Research and Experimentation Tax Credit (R&E Tax Credit). Today, however, many nations provide far more generous tax incentives for research than does the United States. Current tax policy also undermines the effectiveness of the incentive for research, because it is extended periodically on only a temporary basis. Keeping this tax incentive under constant threat of expiration means that businesses planning for long-term research projects have to account for the risk that the credit will not be available, blunting its effectiveness as an incentive. The R&E Tax Credit has been extended temporarily 14 times since its creation in 1981, with some extensions lasting just 6 months. It was even allowed to lapse for 12 months in the mid-1990s, and, as of January 1, 2012, this tax credit had expired again.

Most studies based on historical and cross-country data find that the society-wide returns on R&D are much larger than private returns earned by the investors who fund R&D. Studies have found that social returns to R&D investment to be roughly twice the private returns,[21] a disparity which leads to private sector underinvestment in the absence of policies such as the R&E Tax Credit.

---

[17] For further discussion on the role of tradable sectors and their impact on unemployment and higher-wage jobs, see Michael Spence, *The Impact of Globalization on Income and Employment: The Downside of Integrating Markets*, FOREIGN AFFAIRS, July – Aug. 2011, at 28.

[18] For a review of the U.S. manufacturing sector, see generally DEP'T OF COMMERCE, THE COMPETITIVENESS AND INNOVATION CAPACITY OF THE UNITED STATES (2012).

[19] See, for example, PRESIDENT'S COUNCIL OF ADVISORS ON SCIENCE AND TECHNOLOGY, ENSURING AMERICAN LEADERSHIP IN ADVANCED MANUFACTURING (2011); P. Gary Pisano and Willy C. Shih, *Restoring American Competitiveness*, HARV. BUS. REV. July – Aug. 2009, at 2; Erica Fuchs and Randolph Kirchain, *Design for Location? The Impact of Manufacturing Off-Shore on Technology Competitiveness in the Optoelectronics Industry*, 56 Management Science 2323 (2010); Michael Greenstone, Rick Hornbeck and Enrico Moretti, *Identifying Agglomeration Spillovers: Evidence from Winners and Losers of Large Plant Openings*, 118 J. POL. ECON. 536 (2010).

[20] Bureau of Economic Analysis, U.S. International Trade in Goods and Services, *available at* http://www.bea.gov/international/.

[21] LAURA TYSON AND GREG LINDEN, CTR. FOR AM. PROGRESS, THE CORPORATE R&D TAX CREDIT AND U.S. INNOVATION AND COMPETITIVENESS 7 (2012).

The R&E Tax Credit is also a cost-effective policy for stimulating additional private sector investment. Most recent studies find that each dollar of foregone tax revenue through the R&E Tax Credit causes firms to invest at least a dollar in R&D, with some studies finding a benefit to cost ratio of 2 or 2.96.[22]

Finally, this Framework recognizes that, as we expand manufacturing in the United States, the tax code should encourage doing so in way that is sustainable and that puts the United States in the lead in manufacturing the clean energy technologies of the future. This will create jobs here at home and can also have important spillover benefits. Moving toward a clean energy economy will reduce air and water pollution and enhance our national security by reducing dependence on oil. Cleaner energy will play a crucial role in slowing global climate change, meeting the President's goal of producing 80 percent of our nation's electricity from clean sources by 2035.

President's Framework for Reform

The Framework would strengthen America's manufacturing sector and encourage greater innovation. These are incentives that are important to growth and should have positive spillover effects across the economy. Specifically, the Framework would:

- **Effectively cut the top corporate tax rate on manufacturing income to 25 percent and to an even lower rate for income from advanced manufacturing activities by reforming the domestic production activities deduction.** Reflecting manufacturing's key role in innovation and the intense international competition facing the sector, the President's Framework would reform the current domestic production activities deduction. It would focus the deduction more on manufacturing activity, expand the deduction to 10.7 percent, and increase it even more for advanced manufacturing. This would effectively cut the top corporate tax rate for manufacturing income to 25 percent and even lower for advanced manufacturing.

- **Expand, simplify and make permanent the R&E Tax Credit.** Currently, businesses must choose between using a complex formula for calculating their R&E Tax Credit that provides a 20 percent credit rate for investments over a certain base and a much simpler one that provides a 14 percent credit in excess of a base amount. The complex formula is so outdated that it takes into account the amount of a business's R&D expenses from 1984 to 1988. The President's Framework would increase the rate of the simpler credit to 17 percent, which would make it more attractive and simplify tax filing for businesses. In addition, the credit would be made permanent to increase certainty and effectiveness.

- Extend, consolidate, and enhance **key tax incentives to encourage investment in clean energy.** The President's Framework would make permanent the tax credit for the production of renewable electricity, in order to provide a strong, consistent incentive to encourage investments in renewable energy technologies like wind and solar. As with the R&E Tax Credit, the United States has to date provided only a temporary production tax credit for renewable electricity generation. This approach has created an uncertain investment climate, undermined the effectiveness of our tax expenditures, and hindered the development of a clean energy sector in the United States. In addition, the structure of renewable production and investment tax credits has required many firms to invest in inefficient tax planning through tax equity structures so that they can benefit even when they do not have tax liability in a given year because of a lack of taxable income. The President's Framework would address this issue by making the permanent production tax credit refundable.

---

[22] See Kenneth J. Klassen, Jeffrey A. Pittman, and Margaret P. Reed, *A Cross-National Comparison of R&D Expenditure Decisions: Tax Incentives and Financial Constraints*, 21 CONTEMPORARY ACCOUNTING RESEARCH 639 (2004); Bronwyn H. Hall, *R&D Tax Policy During the Eighties: Success or Failure?*, 7 TAX POL. & THE ECON. 1 (1993).

III. Strengthen the International Tax System to Encourage Domestic Investment

The international provisions of the corporate tax code create opportunities for U.S. companies to reduce their taxes by locating their operations and profits abroad. The tax system is subject to gaming, as corporations manipulate complex tax rules to minimize taxes and, in some cases, shift profit actually earned in the United States to low-tax jurisdictions.

The current U.S. tax system subjects foreign subsidiaries of U.S.-based multinationals to taxes on their overseas income (while allowing a tax credit for foreign taxes paid). However, often corporations do not need to pay taxes in the United States on that income until they repatriate it to the United States, a rule called deferral (since it defers taxation of the income). Many companies reinvest, rather than repatriate, a significant portion of their income overseas and as a result may never face U.S. taxes on much of that income. Although the U.S. tax system is often described as "worldwide" because it taxes U.S. companies on profits earned abroad, opportunities for deferral can make it effectively much closer to a territorial system—a system in which taxes are never paid on foreign income—for many companies.

Because of deferral, U.S. corporations have a significant opportunity to reduce overall taxes paid by shifting profits to low-tax jurisdictions—either by moving their operations and jobs there or by relying on accounting tools and current transfer pricing principles to shift profits there. There is ample evidence that U.S. multinationals' decisions about the choice of where to invest are sensitive to effective tax rates in foreign jurisdictions.[23] There is also strong evidence that corporations use accounting mechanisms to shift profits from where they are actually earned to tax havens and other low-tax jurisdictions.[24] Table 5 shows profits of U.S. corporations reported in select, small countries with very low tax rates. In a number of cases, the amount of profits far exceeds the country's actual output, suggesting the degree to which companies use these countries to shelter profits that may have been earned elsewhere.

TABLE 5: SELECT SMALL COUNTRIES – U.S. FOREIGN COMPANY PROFITS RELATIVE TO GDP

Country	U.S. Foreign Company Profits Relative to GDP
Bahamas	43%
Bermuda	646%
British Virgin Islands	355%
Cayman Islands	547%
Jersey	35%
Liberia	61%
Marshall Islands	340%

Source: JANE G. GRAVELLE, CONG. RES. SERVICE, TAX HAVENS: INTERNATIONAL TAX AVOIDANCE AND EVASION 14 tbl.4 (2010).

---

[23] *See, e.g.*, Rosanne Altshuler and Harry Grubert, *Taxpayer Responses to Competitive Tax Policies and Tax Policy Responses to Competitive Taxpayers: Recent Evidence*, 34 TAX NOTES INT'L 1349 (2004); Harry Grubert and John Mutti, *Taxes, Tariffs and Transfer Pricing in Multinational Corporation Decision Making*, 33 REV. ECON. AND STAT. 285 (1991).

[24] *See supra* notes 11 - 12 and accompanying text.

This distortion in the tax system can lead to inefficient overinvestment abroad and underinvestment in the United States. It can also erode the U.S. tax base, requiring higher tax rates on income that remains taxable in the United States in order to collect the same amount of revenue. Finally, the international tax system is very complex, which not only burdens companies with complicated accounting and tax requirements, but also unfairly benefits the most sophisticated companies which are able to avoid paying taxes by manipulating intricate rules.

There is considerable debate as to how to reform the international tax code. One proposal is to switch to a pure territorial system under which all active foreign income would either be taxed little or not at all in the United States. However, the Administration believes that a pure territorial system could aggravate, rather than ameliorate, many of the problems in the current tax code. If foreign earnings of U.S. multinational corporations are not taxed at all, these firms would have even greater incentives to locate operations abroad or use accounting mechanisms to shift profits out of the United States. Furthermore, such a system could exacerbate the continuing race to the bottom in international tax rates.

At the same time, tax reform should be a foundation to maximize investment, growth and jobs in the United States. It should properly balance the need to reduce tax incentives to locate overseas with the need for U.S. companies to be able to compete overseas; some overseas investments and operations are necessary to serve and expand into foreign markets in ways that benefit U.S. jobs and economic growth. This will be a difficult and complex undertaking, but one guided by the sole criteria of promoting growth in the jobs and standard of living of American workers and their families.

President's Framework for Reform

The President proposes to protect the U.S. tax base and strengthen the international corporate tax system by establishing a new minimum tax on foreign earnings—while repealing deductions for shipping jobs overseas and providing new incentives for bringing jobs back home. Under the President's Framework, reform would:

- **Require companies to pay a minimum tax on overseas profits.** The President believes we must prevent companies from reaping the benefits of locating profits in low-tax countries, put the United States on a more level playing field with our international competitors, and help end the race to the bottom in corporate tax rates.

  Specifically, under the President's proposal, income earned by subsidiaries of U.S. corporations operating abroad must be subject to a minimum rate of tax. This would stop our tax system from generously rewarding companies for moving profits offshore. Thus, foreign income deferred in a low-tax jurisdiction would be subject to immediate U.S. taxation up to the minimum tax rate with a foreign tax credit allowed for income taxes on that income paid to the host country. This minimum tax would be designed to balance the need to stop rewarding tax havens and to prevent a race to the bottom with the goal of keeping U.S. companies on a level playing field with competitors when engaged in activities which, by necessity, must occur in a foreign country.

- **Remove tax deductions for moving productions overseas and provide new incentives for bringing production back to the United States.** The tax code currently allows companies moving operations overseas to deduct their moving expenses—and reduce their taxes in the United States as a result. The President is proposing that companies will no longer be allowed to claim tax deductions for moving their operations abroad. At the same time, to help bring jobs home, the President is proposing to give a 20 percent income tax credit for the expenses of moving operations back into the United States.

- **Other reforms to reduce incentives to shift income and assets overseas**. The Framework would also clean up the international tax code and reduce incentives and opportunities to shift income and assets overseas. For example, as noted above, U.S. companies may use accounting rules or aggressive transfer pricing to shift profit offshore. This is particularly true in the case of profits associated with intangible assets (assets like intellectual property). The Framework would strengthen the international tax rules by taxing currently the excess profits associated with shifting intangibles to low tax jurisdictions. In addition, under current law, U.S. businesses that borrow money and invest overseas can claim the interest they pay as a business expense and take an immediate deduction to reduce their U.S. taxes, even if they pay little or no U.S. taxes on their overseas investment. The Framework would eliminate this tax advantage by requiring that the deduction for the interest expense attributable to overseas investment be delayed until the related income is taxed in the United States.

IV. Simplify and Cut Taxes for America's Small Businesses

America's small businesses face a tax code that is unduly complex. Often, these firms—unlike large businesses—are not engaged in complex transactions, and yet they must spend significant time and resources trying to comply with the tax code. Small businesses are disproportionately burdened with tax compliance, and the cost of this burden is substantial.

In 2004, small businesses devoted between 1.7 and 1.8 billion hours and spent between $15 and $16 billion on tax compliance. On average, each small business devoted about 240 hours complying with the tax code, and spent over $2,000 in tax compliance costs. An overwhelming share of the time burden is due to recordkeeping, while most of the money burden is spent on compensation for paid tax preparers.[25]

For some small businesses, the cost of tax compliance is particularly burdensome. In 2004, 9.7 percent of small business spent over $5,000 in tax compliance and 11.2 percent devoted in excess of 500 hours to compliance. Moreover, for very small businesses, the burden of tax compliance can approach the total amount of taxes paid. For example, for small businesses with between $10,000 and $20,000 in annual receipts, the money burden of compliance is between 6.8 and 7.8 percent of receipts while the time burden amounts to about half—between 51.9 and 52.9 percent—of total receipts. For small business owners with receipts of over $500,000, the average total burden—including the money and time burden—amounted to under 3 percent of total receipts.[26]

The high compliance cost for small businesses is a drag on innovation and entrepreneurship. The large outlays for tax preparers means that small business owners have less capital to reinvest in their companies. The large amount of time spent on recordkeeping and understanding tax provisions means that small business owners have less time and energy for innovation and business development. There are other costs to complexity as well. Frustration with the tax code may eventually lead to weakened compliance and a higher gap between tax revenue owed and tax revenue paid. Moreover, complexity weakens the ability of tax policy to achieve its intended purpose. For example, small business owners might not take advantage of temporary investment incentives—such as the President's proposed expansion of section 179 expensing provisions—if they feel the tax code is too complex to understand overall.

President's Framework for Reform

Tax reform should make tax filing simpler for small businesses and entrepreneurs so that they can focus on growing their businesses rather than filling out tax returns. While some of the base-broadening provisions and other reforms described above would apply to both C-corporations and pass-through entities, the President's Framework includes provisions so that small businesses, including small pass-throughs, receive a net tax cut from reform.

As a way to reduce the tax code's complexity for small businesses and also provide small businesses with tax relief that on net more than offsets any of the base broadening reforms that would otherwise affect them, the President's Framework would:

---

[25] Donald DeLuca et al., *Aggregate Estimates of Small Business Taxpayer Compliance Burden*, IRS RESEARCH BULLETIN, 2007, at 147.
[26] *Id.* The tax burden can also vary by industry, with small businesses in manufacturing, construction, and retail trade devoting more time to compliance than businesses in other industries.

- **Allow small businesses to expense up to $1 million in investments.** Since taking office, the President has secured enactment of temporary increases in the amount of qualified investments that small businesses can expense from $125,000 to $500,000—and, for 2011, temporarily increased that amount to 100 percent of qualified investments with no limit. Under the President's Framework, small businesses would, on a permanent basis, be allowed to expense up to $1,000,000 of qualified investments, which helps offset other changes to the tax base in reform that would affect small businesses. This would provide significant tax relief to America's small businesses and would allow small businesses to avoid the complexity of tracking depreciation schedules.

- **Allow cash accounting on businesses with up to $10 million in gross receipts.** Small businesses with up to $5 million in gross receipts are currently allowed to use this simplified form of accounting. Under the President's Framework, this threshold would increase to $10 million. This simplifies taxes for many more of America's small businesses, since cash accounting can be much easier than accrual accounting—which requires businesses to immediately recognize for income tax purposes their future cash receipts and costs.

In the Budget, the President has also proposed a number of discrete reforms that simplify the tax code for small businesses and provide them with tax relief—and that Congress could act on immediately and should also be included in any fundamental reform. These would:

- **Double the deduction for start-up costs.** This would double the amount of start-up expenses entrepreneurs can immediately deduct from their taxes from $5,000 to $10,000. This offers an immediate incentive for investing in starting up new small businesses, and it also simplifies accounting for small businesses, which must otherwise write off start-up expenses over a period of 15 years.

- **Reform and expand the health insurance tax credit for small businesses.** This credit, created in the Affordable Care Act, helps small businesses afford the cost of health insurance. This reform would allow small businesses with up to 50 workers to qualify for the credit (up from 25), provide a more generous phase-out schedule, and substantially simplify and streamline the tax credit's rules.

V. Restore Fiscal Responsibility

The Federal budget is on an unsustainable course. Even as the economy recovers, the United States carries the legacy of past policies that were not paid for at the time and will continue to drive deficits and debt in the future. Restoring fiscal responsibility will require a set of hard choices to constrain spending, while still making the investments we need in our future. Fiscal responsibility also requires that revenue be increased as part of a balanced approach that asks the wealthiest to contribute more, while protecting the middle class from tax increases. Given the fiscal outlook and the hard choices it requires, the business sector must also be asked to contribute to restoring fiscal sustainability.

President's Framework for Reform

Business tax reform should be fully paid for and be more fiscally responsible than our current system. Under the President's Framework, temporary business tax provisions that are continually extended and have been deficit-financed in the past would either be eliminated or, if they are continued and made permanent, such as the R&E Tax Credit, would be fully paid for within business tax reform. As a result, continuing these items— which, together, represent about $250 billion in costs over the next decade—would no longer add to the deficit under the President's Framework. In fact, the President's balanced approach to restoring fiscal sustainability should improve the investment environment in the United States by helping to keep interest rates low in the years ahead and limiting the crowding out of private investment by government borrowing once the economy recovers.

While a number of the measures that raise revenue in corporate reform—most consequentially, ending accelerated depreciation—raise more revenue in earlier years than they do in later years, the President is committed to corporate tax reform that does not add a dime to the deficit, over the next decade or thereafter. Put simply, the President will only accept business tax reform that is fiscally responsible.

APPENDIX I: Statutory Tax Rate Versus Effective Tax Rate in the United States

The statutory corporate income tax rate offers an incomplete description of investment incentives. The size of the tax base (e.g., the magnitude of depreciation deductions, interest deductions, and special preferences) also matters, as do certain other taxes that corporations must pay, such as property taxes in some countries. A more comprehensive summary measure of the tax burden would include a host of relevant tax rates, deductions, and credits. These more comprehensive measures suggest that the U.S. tax system is more in line with that of our major competitors in terms of effective tax rates, as opposed to a comparison based on statutory corporate income tax rates alone.

One such measure is the effective marginal corporate tax rate (EMTR). The EMTR is the hypothetical corporate tax rate that, if applied to economic income, would offer the same investment incentive on a new, just barely profitable, investment, as does the combination of tax rates, depreciation deductions, interest deductions, and, in some cases, other features that characterize the actual tax system. Generally, the lower the EMTR, the greater the incentive to invest.

The second column of Table A1 shows the EMTR in G-7 countries, including the United States. The calculations are for a representative mix of physical assets (equipment, buildings, and inventory), financed using a combination of debt and equity.

The United States' EMTR is close to, and actually is slightly below, the average for the other G-7 countries, despite the United States' relatively high statutory corporate income tax rate. Two factors largely account for this difference. One factor is the relatively high property and wealth taxes that are imposed by other G-7 countries. The second is debt finance and the value of the interest deduction. The high statutory tax rate in the United States combined with a full deduction of nominal interest results in a very low EMTR on U.S. debt-financed investment. In contrast, the interest deduction does less to lower the EMTR in other countries, which tend to have lower statutory corporate income tax rates and some of which restrict the deductibility of interest.

The effective average corporate tax rate (EATR) is an alternative summary measure of the effect of taxes on investment incentives. This measure is a weighted combination of the EMTR and the statutory corporate income tax rate. It is intended to better capture investment incentives for lumpy, large, discrete investments, often involving intangibles such as patents and trademarks, on which firms might expect to earn pure profits, rather than just the normal return. On such profitable investments, tax incentives such as accelerated depreciation, do not matter, while the statutory tax rate has a large effect. To the extent that the investment under consideration is a mix of assets earning pure profits and assets earning a normal return, the EATR can be relevant for measuring investment incentives. Because such investments—e.g., a factory designed to manufacture a product based on a patent—may be typical for a multinational corporation, the EATR frequently is used as a measure of the tax incentives that affect firms' decisions on where to locate investments.[27] In contrast, the EMTR is regarded as an appropriate measure of the effect of taxes on the decision about how big to make a factory in a given country, conditional on deciding to build the factory in that country.

---

[27] Others question the relevance of this measure because the source of the profit is not explicitly considered. If the source of the apparent profit is a risk premium, then it is not clear that taxes would impose any burden on it because the disincentive effect of the tax on the expected returns is offset by the tax's reduction in the variance in the return (reduction in the risk borne by the investor). *See* JANE G. GRAVELLE, CONG. RES. SERVICE, INTERNATIONAL CORPORATE TAX RATE COMPARISONS AND POLICY IMPLICATIONS (2011).

The United States has an EATR that is somewhat above that for most other G-7 countries. This reflects the importance of the statutory corporate income tax rate (including subnational tax rates and surcharges) in the calculations. Nonetheless, because of the United States's relatively low EMTR, the United States is closer to the G-7 mean when considering EATRs than when looking at statutory corporate income tax rates alone.

TABLE A1: G-7 STATUTORY AND EFFECTIVE CORPORATE TAX RATES (IN PERCENT) FOR 2011

	Statutory Corporate Tax Rate[c]	Overall Effective Tax Rates (Corporate Level)	
		Effective Marginal Tax Rate[b]	Effective Average Tax Rate[b]
Canada	27.6	33.0	29.6
France	34.4	28.3	32.3
Germany	30.2	23.3	27.9
Italy	31.3	24.0	28.9
Japan	39.5	42.9	41.0
United Kingdom	26.0	32.3	28.3
United States[d]	39.2	29.2	35.7
G-7 Average excluding the U.S.[a]	32.3	31.9	32.6

Source: U.S. Department of the Treasury, Office of Tax Analysis.

Notes: EMTR = effective marginal tax rates; EATR = effective average tax rates.

a. The G-7 Average is calculated using 2010 gross domestic product (in current US dollars) as weights.

b. The overall EMTR is calculated as the difference between an average cost of capital (across type of asset and type of finance) and an after-tax real rate of return. In calculating an average cost of capital across type of finance, Devereux, et al. (2009) use weights of 65 percent for retained earnings and new equity combined, and 35 percent for debt.

c. Effective statutory corporate tax rates are obtained using tax parameters from Section A of Devereux, et al. (2009), "Project for the EU Commission, Effective Tax Levels Using the Devereux/Griffith Methodology," TAXUD/2008/CC/099, Report 2009, available at http://ec.europa.eu/taxation_customs/resources/documents/publications/studies/etr_company.pdf. The tax parameters used to calculate the effective statutory corporate tax rates are supplemented with data from the OECD Tax Database. The tax parameters used to calculate the PV of depreciation are supplemented with data from the PricewaterhouseCoopers Worldwide Tax Summaries and the International Bureau of Fiscal Documentation online.

d. EMTRs and EATRs for machinery do not reflect the 100-percent bonus depreciation for property placed in service after September 8, 2010 and before January 1, 2012.

The effective statutory corporate tax rates include top statutory corporate income tax rates, surcharges, and local profits tax rates (nominal). The EMTR and EATR also include effective real estate tax rates and net wealth tax rates. The same real rate of return, inflation rate, and economic depreciation rates are used for all countries. As a result, any differences in EMTR and EATR reflect differences in tax regimes.

In sum, the analysis of EMTRs and EATRs suggests that the U.S. tax system offers investment incentives that are within the range of those offered by other G-7 countries.

Note that, as explained above in Section II, this does not argue against the need for base broadening, rate reducing tax reform. Using tax expenditures and tax incentives to lower the effective rate can be a less effective way at promoting efficient investment in the United States than a broader base with a lower rate.

In this regard, when it comes to the EMTR and EATR, analysis shows that U.S. taxes are lower on investments that just break even (as measured by the EMTR) than on more profitable investments (as measured by the EATR). Corporate reform that broadened the tax base while simultaneously cutting the statutory corporate tax rate could be broadly consistent with maintaining the current U.S. EMTR, while reducing the EATR. As explained earlier, the EATR is often considered to reflect the effect of taxes on the location of an investment, while the EMTR is considered an indicator of the effect of taxes on the scale of an investment. Thus, in addition to the benefits already discussed in Section II of broadening the tax base, tax reform could, in this way, be effective in attracting highly profitable investment projects to the United States.

APPENDIX II: Effective Marginal Tax Rates Including Individual Income Taxes

Other tables in this paper show effective tax rates at the corporate level. They do not include individual income taxes. Table A2 below also includes individual income taxes, and, with that included, the same biases discussed earlier in this paper remain. Marginal tax rates vary significantly by asset type, organizational type, and source of financing.

TABLE A2: EFFECTIVE MARGINAL TAX RATES ON NEW INVESTMENT (IN PERCENT)
(INCLUDING CORPORATE INCOME TAX AND INDIVIDUAL INCOME TAX)

Entity	Current-law Baseline
Business	30.1
Corporate Business	32.3
Asset Type	
Equipment[a]	27.3
Structures[b]	32.7
Land[c]	39.0
Inventories[c,d]	41.9
Intangibles[e]	6.2
Financing	
Debt-financed	-4.4
Equity-financed	36.8
Noncorporate Business	26.4
Asset Type	
Equipment[a]	18.7
Structures[b]	24.6
Land[c]	30.6
Inventories[c,d]	33.8
Intangibles[e]	-3.1
Owner-occupied Housing	-3.5
Economy-wide	21.3

Source: U.S. Department of the Treasury, Office of Tax Analysis

The effective marginal tax rates (EMTR) shown combine the statutory corporate income tax rate, accelerated tax depreciation, the business interest deduction, the home mortgage interest deduction, and various individual-level taxes (including a noncorporate business income tax rate). The individual-level taxes are an average of 2013-2022 income-weighted federal marginal tax rates from Treasury's

Individual Tax Model. They are consistent with a current-law baseline, implying that they assume the expiration in 2012 of recently extended provisions of the 2001 and 2003 tax acts. Those provisions include lower marginal tax rates on ordinary income, preferential tax rates on capital gains and dividend income, an increase in the child tax credit, and marriage penalty relief.

a.   Includes both nonresidential and residential equipment.
b.   Includes nonresidential, tenant-occupied, and owner-occupied structures.
c.   The economic depreciation rate is set to zero and no tax depreciation is included when calculating effective marginal tax rates for land and inventories.
d.   For inventories, the real before-tax rate of return is a weighted average of the cost of capital under last-in-first-out (LIFO) accounting and first-in-first-out (FIFO) accounting.
e.   The intangible assets include research and development capital.

www.ingramcontent.com/pod-product-compliance
Lightning Source LLC
Chambersburg PA
CBHW080404290526
45790CB00009BA/3697